anythink

D0788299

Designer Dogs

Goldadors

by Ruth Owen

PowerKiDS
press

New York

Published in 2015 by The Rosen Publishing Group, Inc.
29 East 21st Street, New York, NY 10010

First Edition

Produced for Rosen by Ruby Tuesday Books Ltd
Editor for Ruby Tuesday Books Ltd: Mark J. Sachner
US Editor: Joshua Shadowens
Designer: Emma Randall

Photo Credits:
Cover, 4 (left), 4 (center), 8–9, 10–11, 12–13, 14–15, 19, 30 © Shutterstock;
1, 3, 4 (right), 7, 16–17, 18, 22–23 © Warren Photographic; 5, 21, 25, 28
© Alamy; 27 © Canine Companions for Independence; 29 © Chula Vista
Fire Department.

Library of Congress Cataloging-in-Publication Data

Owen, Ruth, 1967– author.
 Goldadors / by Ruth Owen. — 1st ed.
     pages cm. — (Designer dogs)
 Includes index.
 ISBN 978-1-4777-7039-9 (library binding) — ISBN 978-1-4777-7040-5 (pbk.) —
 ISBN 978-1-4777-7041-2 (6-pack)
 1. Goldador—Juvenile literature. 2. Working dogs—Juvenile literature.
 3. Dogs—Juvenile literature. I. Title.
 SF429.G62O94 2015
 636.73—dc23

                                            2014006012

Manufactured in the United States of America

CPSIA Compliance Information: Batch #WS14PK8: For Further Information contact Rosen Publishing, New York, New York at 1-800-237-9932

Contents

woof oo

Meet a Goldador

What is super friendly, super smart, loves to play, but also likes to work? The answer is a goldador.

When a golden retriever and a Labrador retriever have puppies together, they make goldadors. A goldador is a **crossbreed** dog. That's because it is a cross, or mixture, of two different dog **breeds**.

Most goldadors are pet dogs, but others work as guide dogs or **assistance dogs**.

Adult golden retriever

Adult Labrador retriever

Goldador puppy

The name "goldador" is made up from the words "golden" and "Labrador" in the names of the parent breeds. Goldadors are also sometimes called glabs or retrievadors.

An adult goldador

Designing a Super Pooch

Golden retrievers and Labrador retrievers are two of the friendliest, most easy-going dog breeds. These dogs are also very smart and can be trained to do important jobs. So dog **breeders** decided to put these two breeds together and make friendly, intelligent, easy-to-train goldadors.

Dogs, such as goldadors, that are created from two existing dog breeds have been nicknamed "designer dogs." That's because they were designed, or invented, by people.

Golden retrievers have also been bred with poodles to make a designer dog breed called goldendoodles. Labrador retrievers and poodles make labradoodles.

Two goldador puppies

Meet the Parents: Golden Retrievers

Golden retrievers are one of the most popular dog breeds in the United States.

Every year, the American Kennel Club makes a list of how many dogs are owned in each breed. The 2013 list included 177 different breeds. Golden retrievers were the third most popular breed on the list!

Golden retrievers have thick, shiny coats that can range from a pale, whitish-gold color to a dark, orange-gold color.

Adult golden retriever size

Height to shoulder = up to 24 inches (61 cm)

A golden retriever taking part in an agility competition

Golden retriever puppies

An adult golden retriever usually weighs between 55 and 75 pounds (25–34 kg).

Meet the Parents: Working Retrievers

Golden retrievers were first bred in Scotland in the 1800s. This breed was created to help hunters.

In the 1800s, people hunted birds, such as pheasants, and waterfowl, such as ducks, for food and for sport. Hunters shot the birds from a distance. Then the hunters' gun dogs, such as golden retrievers, would retrieve the dead birds and carry them back to their owners. Often the dogs had to retrieve birds from ponds or lakes.

A pet golden retriever retrieving a ball

To keep them warm and dry in water, golden retrievers were bred with a double coat. They have a thick undercoat for warmth and a long, waterproof outer coat.

Meet the Parents: Labrador Retrievers

Just like the golden retriever, Labrador retrievers were originally bred as working dogs.

Hundreds of years ago, these dogs worked with fishermen in Newfoundland, Canada. Labradors were trained to swim to fishing nets that were full of fish. Then the dogs would catch hold of the nets with their mouths and drag them into shore.

Today, some Labradors work as gun dogs. They retrieve birds and other small animals for their owners during hunting trips.

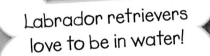

Labrador retrievers love to be in water!

A Labrador's mouth
is so soft and gentle that it can carry a
dead animal without damaging it. It can
even carry an egg without breaking it!

13

Meet the Parents: Popular and Smart

According to the American Kennel Club list, Labrador retrievers have been the number one most popular dog in the United States for the past 20 years!

Most Labradors and golden retrievers are pet dogs, but some have important jobs. Both breeds are trained to be guide dogs for the blind. Some work at airports, using their sense of smell to sniff for **illegal drugs** in passengers' luggage. Some are even trained to be search and rescue dogs. These dogs track people who are lost in **wilderness** areas such as forests.

Adult Labrador
retriever size

Height to shoulder =
up to 24 inches (61 cm)

Weight =
55 to 90 pounds
(25–41 kg)

Labrador retrievers come in three different colors, yellow, black, and chocolate.

Black Labrador retriever mom

Yellow puppy

Chocolate puppies

Goldador Puppies

A goldador puppy may have a golden retriever mom and a Labrador retriever dad, or the other way around. The mother dog can give birth to up to 10 goldador puppies at one time.

A one-week-old goldador puppy

Like all newborn puppies, the tiny goldadors spend the first four weeks of their lives sleeping and drinking milk from mom. Once they get to four weeks old, though, the pups have grown stronger and have lots of energy. Then it's time for puppy mayhem as 10 little goldadors chase each other and play fight.

A goldador puppy must stay with its mom for the first eight weeks. Then it is old enough to go to live with a new human family.

Gorgeous Goldadors

Just like its water dog parents, a goldador has a thick double coat of hair. It has a soft undercoat and a short, thick, straight outer coat.

A goldador's hair is usually yellow to reddish-gold. Sometimes, however, despite its name, a goldador may have a black coat **inherited** from its Labrador retriever family.

A fully grown goldador usually weighs between 60 and 80 pounds (27–36 kg). It can grow up to 24 inches (61 cm) at the shoulder.

Two golden and one black goldador puppies

An adult goldador

19

Goldador Personalities

Goldadors love their people and want to be with their owners at all times.

These intelligent dogs need to keep their brains busy by doing work or learning new things. A pet goldador can be trained to do tricks. It can even be trained to help out with tasks such as fetching the newspaper from the front yard.

Goldadors are sensitive dogs who want to please. So reward them when they get a task right, but don't tell them off if they get it wrong. Being told off will damage their confidence.

Goldadors are much too friendly to be guard dogs. They are good watchdogs, though, and will bark to let you know someone is near your home.

Like its mom and dad, a goldador loves water!

21

Pet Goldadors

Goldadors like to eat. A lot! It's important, therefore, that a pet goldador gets lots of exercise to stop it from becoming overweight. A 30-minute walk or a game of retrieving, or fetching, a toy is just perfect.

Goldadors love to be outdoors and enjoy hiking with their owners. Once a goldador is fully grown and at full strength, it will even enjoy going jogging with its owner.

A goldador sheds, or loses, hair from its coat. A weekly brush helps keep the loose hair under control.

A goldador puppy

Goldadors get along well with other breeds of dogs and other pets—even cats!

23

Goldador Guide Dogs

A guide dog is trained to lead its owner wherever the person needs to go. Just like their parent breeds, goldadors are people-pleasing dogs, so becoming a busy guide dog is a great life.

If a goldador puppy pays attention to people and shows confidence, it may be chosen to train for this work. Guide dogs learn to stop at roadside curbs. They are trained to lead their owners up and down stairs and into elevators. They also guide their owners onto buses and trains.

A guide dog learns to lie quietly while traveling on buses or trains. It must also sit or lie patiently beside its owner all day when its owner is at work.

This goldador (right) is riding on a bus as part of its guide dog training.

Goldador Assistance Dogs

Assistance dogs are trained to help people with physical disabilities. Super-smart, people-loving goldadors are just the right breed for doing this work.

An assistance dog can be trained to do many tasks. It might pull its owner's wheelchair and open doors for its owner to pass through. The dog can switch lights on and off and press buttons on elevators. An assistance dog is also trained to pick up objects that its owner drops and to retrieve objects that its owner needs.

A goldador can be trained to become a hearing assist dog for a person who is deaf. When the dog hears a noise, such as a smoke alarm or the doorbell, it tells its owner by touching him or her with its paw or nose.

Hiley the goldador assistance dog with her owner Tommy

Fire Detection Dogs

Some dogs use their sense of smell to get a job with a fire department.

Fires in buildings often start by accident. Sometimes, however, people set fire to a building deliberately. Then the fire department must investigate how the fire got started.

Accelerant detection dogs visit burned-out buildings. They are trained to sniff for accelerants, such as gasoline, that may have been used to make a fire burn. Goldadors, Labradors, and retrievers can all be trained to do this work.

Here, Cali, the accelerant detection goldador, is practicing sniffing for gasoline in some cans.

Once an accelerant detection dog finds the scent of gasoline in a building, it sits and points its nose at the spot. Then it receives a food treat from its human partner.

Cali and her human partner, Darin, enter a burned-out building

Glossary

accelerant
(ik-SEH-luh-rent)
A substance, such as gasoline or lighter fuel, that is used to light a fire, or to make a fire burn faster.

assistance dogs
(uh-SIS-tints DAWGZ)
Dogs that are trained to help people who have a disability or who need comfort and attention.

breeders
(BREE-derz) People who breed animals, such as dogs, and sell them.

breeds (BREEDZ)
Different types of dogs. The word "breed" is also used to describe the act of mating two dogs in order for them to have puppies.

crossbreed
(KROS-breed) A type of dog created from two different breeds.

illegal drugs
(ih-LEE-gul DRUGZ)
Types of drugs that are
against the law to use
or sell.

inherited (in-HER-it-ed)
Having a quality, such
as hair color or size, that
has been passed on by
parents and may come
from ancestors, which
are relatives that lived
long ago.

wilderness
(WIL-dur-nis) A wild area
of land, such as a forest,
that is far from any
towns or cities.

Websites
Due to the changing nature
of Internet links, PowerKids Press has
developed an online list of websites related to the
subject of this book. This site is updated regularly.
Please use this link to access the list:

www.powerkidslinks.com/ddog/gold/

Read More

Larrew, Brekka Hervey. *Golden Retrievers*. All About Dogs. Mankato, MN: Capstone Press, 2009.

Nelson, Maria. *Labrador Retrievers*. Great Big Dogs. New York: Gareth Stevens, 2012.

Wood, Alix. *Animal Handler*. The World's Coolest Jobs. New York: PowerKids Press, 2014.

Index